Novel Assistant

Novel Assistant Publishing

Ireland

All rights reserved. No part of this publication may be reproduced, distributed, or transmitted in any form or by any means, including photocopying, recording, or other electronic or mechanical methods, without the prior written permission of the publisher, except in the case of brief quotations embodied in critical reviews and certain other non-commercial uses permitted by copyright law. For permission requests, email to the publisher, addressed "Attention: Permissions Coordinator,"
at the following website:

www.novelassistantpublishing.com

This book is to be used as a guide and to be helpful to authors for preplanning their novel writing. Novel Assistant will not be held accountable in any way for author's works.

Copyright © A.J. Mathews 2017

All rights reserved.

ISBN- 978-1-9998817-0-2

Novel Assistant

This simple to use journal is your hands on, take everywhere, guard with your life novel assistant. This book is your planning, or what we like to call your pre-work before you actually start writing your novel.

If you are asking yourself where to start or find yourself stuck in the writing process, let Novel Assistant serve as a working guide to help you complete your dream of finishing a novel. Each book is complete with:

Title Page

Story Summary

Character Development

Chapter Planning

Story Timelines

Yearly Writing Calendar

and

Notes

Keep all of your novel planning in one place. We have created an organized journal where you can plan your very best story. Designed for beginning writers, Novel Assistant has been especially created to keep you focused so that you can plan your novel.

Take this book with you everywhere. Leave it beside you as you sleep. Take it with you as you travel, on the train or to the coffee shop. You never know when a great idea will pop into your head or even your dreams. Develop your characters and plot out your chapters within one place.

Everyone has a story to tell...**Especially YOU!!!**

Contents

Introduction 1

Title Page 3

Story Summary 4

Character Development 11

Chapter Plotting 135

Yearly Writing Calendar 267

Notes 280

INTRODUCTION

Novel Assistant has been divided into the following sections:

Title Page - This is where your novel begins. Here you can write down the title of your novel, your name as the author, and genre of your book.

Story Summary - In this section, write down the basic idea of your novel. Keep it simple as your story will unfold in your chapter plotting section.

Character List - Once you have chosen the characters for your novel, write down their names in the character list section.

Character Development - Take each character and bring them to life in this section of your book. There are 31 interview questions for up to 20 characters. Interview each character as if they are sitting in front of you. Really think about how they would answer. Then, turn things around and answer questions in the author notes section. Get to know your characters. Take a walk around in their shoes. Fully developing each character will make a huge difference when writing your novel. Be creative and let your imagination flow.

Timeline - After you have a story line in mind, jot it down on your timeline. This is a good way to keep focused when plotting out your chapters. You may want to master your timeline on a separate piece of paper before writing it in your book.

Chapter Planning - Now that you have your characters developed, plan out each chapter in this section. Start by giving each chapter a title. Create the date, time, setting, characters, voice and point of view of each chapter. Then, write down the basic summary of up to thirty-two chapters.

Writing Calendar - After you have developed your characters and completed plotting each chapter you are ready to start writing. Stay focused on your writing with your one year writing calendar. Keep track of what chapter you are working on, your estimated daily word count, and your actual word count. If you write 250 words per day, you will have 91,250 words in one year.

Notes – Need more writing space? Check the back of your book!

Title Page

(Book Title)

(Author)

(Genre)

Story Summary

Story Summary

Story Summary

Story Summary

Story Summary

Story Summary

Character Development

Character List

1. _____
   _____

2. _____
   _____

3. _____
   _____

4. _____
   _____

5. _____
   _____

6. _____
   _____

7. _____
   _____

8. _____
   _____

9. _____
   _____

10. _____
    _____

11. _____
_____

12. _____
_____

13. _____
_____

14. _____
_____

15. _____
_____

16. _____
_____

17. _____
_____

18. _____
_____

19. _____
_____

20. _____
_____

Character One

1) What is your full name?

_____

2) How old are you and what is your gender?

_____

3) What colour is your hair; your eyes; your skin?

_____

4) Describe your physical appearance in further detail:

_____

_____

_____

5) Describe your personality:

_____

_____

_____

6) Where are you from; where did you grow up?

_____

_____

_____

7) Where do you live now?

_____

_____

_____

8) Who are your parents?

_____
_____
_____

9) Who are your grandparents and what is their ancestral background?

_____
_____
_____

10) Who are your friends and what do you do together?

_____
_____
_____

11) If you are an adult, where do you work?

_____
_____
_____

12) If you are a child, where do you go to school?

_____
_____
_____

13) What are your likes/hobbies?

_____
_____
_____

14) What are your dislikes?

_____
_____
_____

15) Do you have a love interest?

_____
_____
_____

16) What makes that person special to you?

_____
_____
_____

17) What is your view on the world?

_____
_____
_____

18) Describe your childhood:

_____
_____
_____

19) What do you care about?

_____
_____
_____

20) What is your biggest fear?

_____

_____

21) Do you have any secrets?

_____

_____

22) How would you define yourself?

_____

_____

23) What is the best thing that has ever happened to you?

_____

_____

24) What is the worst thing that has ever happened to you?

_____

_____

25) What would you like to accomplish in life?

_____

_____

_____

26) What do you dream about?

_____
_____
_____

27) Are you a clean or messy person? Why?

_____
_____
_____

28) What makes you laugh?

_____
_____
_____

29) What shocks or offends you?

_____
_____
_____

30) Share a funny fact about yourself:

_____
_____
_____

31) Share a deep fact about yourself:

_____
_____
_____

Author Notes on this Character

Pretend you are alone with this character. Describe them here:

_____
_____
_____
_____
_____

Write 10 words about this character as if you have known them their whole life:

_____
_____
_____
_____
_____

Now, step into this characters shoes. What do they want to accomplish in your story?

_____
_____
_____
_____
_____

Character Two

1) What is your full name?

_____

2) How old are you and what is your gender?

_____

3) What colour is your hair; your eyes; your skin?

_____

4) Describe your physical appearance in further detail:

_____

_____

_____

5) Describe your personality:

_____

_____

_____

6) Where are you from; where did you grow up?

_____

_____

_____

7) Where do you live now?

_____

_____

_____

8) Who are your parents?

_____

_____

9) Who are your grandparents and what is their ancestral background?

_____

_____

10) Who are your friends and what do you do together?

_____

_____

11) If you are an adult, where do you work?

_____

_____

12) If you are a child, where do you go to school?

_____

_____

13) What are your likes/hobbies?

_____

_____

14) What are your dislikes?

_____
_____
_____

15) Do you have a love interest?

_____
_____
_____

16) What makes that person special to you?

_____
_____
_____

17) What is your view on the world?

_____
_____
_____

18) Describe your childhood:

_____
_____
_____

19) What do you care about?

_____
_____
_____

20) What is your biggest fear?

21) Do you have any secrets?

22) How would you define yourself?

23) What is the best thing that has ever happened to you?

24) What is the worst thing that has ever happened to you?

25) What would you like to accomplish in life?

26) What do you dream about?

_____

_____

_____

27) Are you a clean or messy person? Why?

_____

_____

_____

28) What makes you laugh?

_____

_____

_____

29) What shocks or offends you?

_____

_____

_____

30) Share a funny fact about yourself:

_____

_____

_____

31) Share a deep fact about yourself:

_____

_____

_____

Author Notes on this Character

Pretend you are alone with this character. Describe them here:

_____
_____
_____
_____
_____

Write 10 words about this character as if you have known them their whole life:

_____
_____
_____
_____
_____

Now, step into this characters shoes. What do they want to accomplish in your story?

_____
_____
_____
_____
_____

Character Three

1) What is your full name?

_____

2) How old are you and what is your gender?

_____

3) What colour is your hair; your eyes; your skin?

_____

4) Describe your physical appearance in further detail:

_____

_____

_____

5) Describe your personality:

_____

_____

_____

6) Where are you from; where did you grow up?

_____

_____

_____

7) Where do you live now?

_____

_____

_____

8) Who are your parents?

_____

_____

_____

9) Who are your grandparents and what is their ancestral background?

_____

_____

_____

10) Who are your friends and what do you do together?

_____

_____

_____

11) If you are an adult, where do you work?

_____

_____

_____

12) If you are a child, where do you go to school?

_____

_____

13) What are your likes/hobbies?

_____

_____

_____

14) What are your dislikes?

_____
_____
_____

15) Do you have a love interest?

_____
_____
_____

16) What makes that person special to you?

_____
_____
_____

17) What is your view on the world?

_____
_____
_____

18) Describe your childhood:

_____
_____
_____

19) What do you care about?

_____
_____
_____

20) What is your biggest fear?

_____

_____

_____

21) Do you have any secrets?

_____

_____

_____

22) How would you define yourself?

_____

_____

_____

23) What is the best thing that has ever happened to you?

_____

_____

_____

24) What is the worst thing that has ever happened to you?

_____

_____

_____

25) What would you like to accomplish in life?

_____

_____

_____

26) What do you dream about?

27) Are you a clean or messy person? Why?

28) What makes you laugh?

29) What shocks or offends you?

30) Share a funny fact about yourself:

31) Share a deep fact about yourself:

Author Notes on this Character

Pretend you are alone with this character. Describe them here:

_____
_____
_____
_____
_____

Write 10 words about this character as if you have known them their whole life:

_____
_____
_____
_____
_____

Now, step into this characters shoes. What do they want to accomplish in your story?

_____
_____
_____
_____
_____

Character Four

1) What is your full name?

_____

2) How old are you and what is your gender?

_____

3) What colour is your hair; your eyes; your skin?

_____

4) Describe your physical appearance in further detail:

_____

_____

_____

5) Describe your personality:

_____

_____

_____

6) Where are you from; where did you grow up?

_____

_____

_____

7) Where do you live now?

_____

_____

_____

8) Who are your parents?

_____

_____

_____

9) Who are your grandparents and what is their ancestral background?

_____

_____

_____

10) Who are your friends and what do you do together?

_____

_____

_____

11) If you are an adult, where do you work?

_____

_____

_____

12) If you are a child, where do you go to school?

_____

_____

_____

13) What are your likes/hobbies?

_____

_____

_____

14) What are your dislikes?

_____
_____
_____

15) Do you have a love interest?

_____
_____
_____

16) What makes that person special to you?

_____
_____
_____

17) What is your view on the world?

_____
_____
_____

18) Describe your childhood:

_____
_____
_____

19) What do you care about?

_____
_____
_____

20) What is your biggest fear?

_____
_____

21) Do you have any secrets?

_____
_____

22) How would you define yourself?

_____
_____

23) What is the best thing that has ever happened to you?

_____
_____

24) What is the worst thing that has ever happened to you?

_____
_____

25) What would you like to accomplish in life?

_____
_____

26) What do you dream about?

27) Are you a clean or messy person? Why?

28) What makes you laugh?

29) What shocks or offends you?

30) Share a funny fact about yourself:

31) Share a deep fact about yourself:

Author Notes on this Character

Pretend you are alone with this character. Describe them here:

_____
_____
_____
_____
_____

Write 10 words about this character as if you have known them their whole life:

_____
_____
_____
_____
_____

Now, step into this characters shoes. What do they want to accomplish in your story?

_____
_____
_____
_____
_____

Character Five

1) What is your full name?

_____

2) How old are you and what is your gender?

_____

3) What colour is your hair; your eyes; your skin?

_____

4) Describe your physical appearance in further detail:

_____

_____

_____

5) Describe your personality:

_____

_____

_____

6) Where are you from; where did you grow up?

_____

_____

_____

7) Where do you live now?

_____

_____

_____

8) Who are your parents?

_____

_____

_____

9) Who are your grandparents and what is their ancestral background?

_____

_____

_____

10) Who are your friends and what do you do together?

_____

_____

_____

11) If you are an adult, where do you work?

_____

_____

_____

12) If you are a child, where do you go to school?

_____

_____

_____

13) What are your likes/hobbies?

_____

_____

_____

14) What are your dislikes?

15) Do you have a love interest?

16) What makes that person special to you?

17) What is your view on the world?

18) Describe your childhood:

19) What do you care about?

20) What is your biggest fear?

_____

_____

21) Do you have any secrets?

_____

_____

22) How would you define yourself?

_____

_____

23) What is the best thing that has ever happened to you?

_____

_____

24) What is the worst thing that has ever happened to you?

_____

_____

25) What would you like to accomplish in life?

_____

_____

26) What do you dream about?

_____
_____
_____

27) Are you a clean or messy person? Why?

_____
_____
_____

28) What makes you laugh?

_____
_____
_____

29) What shocks or offends you?

_____
_____
_____

30) Share a funny fact about yourself:

_____
_____
_____

31) Share a deep fact about yourself:

_____
_____
_____

Author Notes on this Character

Pretend you are alone with this character. Describe them here:

_____
_____
_____
_____
_____

Write 10 words about this character as if you have known them their whole life:

_____
_____
_____
_____
_____

Now, step into this characters shoes. What do they want to accomplish in your story?

_____
_____
_____
_____
_____

Character Six

1) What is your full name?

___

2) How old are you and what is your gender?

___

3) What colour is your hair; your eyes; your skin?

___

4) Describe your physical appearance in further detail:

___

___

___

5) Describe your personality:

___

___

___

6) Where are you from; where did you grow up?

___

___

___

7) Where do you live now?

___

___

___

8) Who are your parents?

_____

_____

_____

9) Who are your grandparents and what is their ancestral background?

_____

_____

_____

10) Who are your friends and what do you do together?

_____

_____

_____

11) If you are an adult, where do you work?

_____

_____

_____

12) If you are a child, where do you go to school?

_____

_____

_____

13) What are your likes/hobbies?

_____

_____

_____

14) What are your dislikes?

_____
_____
_____

15) Do you have a love interest?

_____
_____
_____

16) What makes that person special to you?

_____
_____
_____

17) What is your view on the world?

_____
_____
_____

18) Describe your childhood:

_____
_____
_____

19) What do you care about?

_____
_____
_____

20) What is your biggest fear?

_____

_____

_____

21) Do you have any secrets?

_____

_____

_____

22) How would you define yourself?

_____

_____

_____

23) What is the best thing that has ever happened to you?

_____

_____

_____

24) What is the worst thing that has ever happened to you?

_____

_____

_____

25) What would you like to accomplish in life?

_____

_____

_____

26) What do you dream about?

_____

_____

_____

27) Are you a clean or messy person? Why?

_____

_____

_____

28) What makes you laugh?

_____

_____

_____

29) What shocks or offends you?

_____

_____

_____

30) Share a funny fact about yourself:

_____

_____

_____

31) Share a deep fact about yourself:

_____

_____

_____

Author Notes on this Character

Pretend you are alone with this character. Describe them here:

_____
_____
_____
_____
_____

Write 10 words about this character as if you have known them their whole life:

_____
_____
_____
_____
_____

Now, step into this characters shoes. What do they want to accomplish in your story?

_____
_____
_____
_____
_____

CHARACTER SEVEN

1) What is your full name?

_____

2) How old are you and what is your gender?

_____

3) What colour is your hair; your eyes; your skin?

_____

4) Describe your physical appearance in further detail:

_____

_____

_____

5) Describe your personality:

_____

_____

_____

6) Where are you from; where did you grow up?

_____

_____

_____

7) Where do you live now?

_____

_____

_____

8) Who are your parents?

_____

_____

_____

9) Who are your grandparents and what is their ancestral background?

_____

_____

_____

10) Who are your friends and what do you do together?

_____

_____

_____

11) If you are an adult, where do you work?

_____

_____

_____

12) If you are a child, where do you go to school?

_____

_____

_____

13) What are your likes/hobbies?

_____

_____

_____

14) What are your dislikes?

_____
_____
_____

15) Do you have a love interest?

_____
_____
_____

16) What makes that person special to you?

_____
_____
_____

17) What is your view on the world?

_____
_____
_____

18) Describe your childhood:

_____
_____
_____

19) What do you care about?

_____
_____
_____

20) What is your biggest fear?

_____

_____

21) Do you have any secrets?

_____

_____

22) How would you define yourself?

_____

_____

23) What is the best thing that has ever happened to you?

_____

_____

24) What is the worst thing that has ever happened to you?

_____

_____

25) What would you like to accomplish in life?

_____

_____

26) What do you dream about?

27) Are you a clean or messy person? Why?

28) What makes you laugh?

29) What shocks or offends you?

30) Share a funny fact about yourself:

31) Share a deep fact about yourself:

AUTHOR NOTES ON THIS CHARACTER

Pretend you are alone with this character. Describe them here:

_____
_____
_____
_____
_____

Write 10 words about this character as if you have known them their whole life:

_____
_____
_____
_____
_____

Now, step into this characters shoes. What do they want to accomplish in your story?

_____
_____
_____
_____
_____

Character Eight

1) What is your full name?

___

2) How old are you and what is your gender?

___

3) What colour is your hair; your eyes; your skin?

___

4) Describe your physical appearance in further detail:

___

___

___

5) Describe your personality:

___

___

___

6) Where are you from; where did you grow up?

___

___

___

7) Where do you live now?

___

___

___

8) Who are your parents?

_____

_____

_____

9) Who are your grandparents and what is their ancestral background?

_____

_____

_____

10) Who are your friends and what do you do together?

_____

_____

_____

11) If you are an adult, where do you work?

_____

_____

_____

12) If you are a child, where do you go to school?

_____

_____

_____

13) What are your likes/hobbies?

_____

_____

_____

14) What are your dislikes?

_____
_____
_____

15) Do you have a love interest?

_____
_____
_____

16) What makes that person special to you?

_____
_____
_____

17) What is your view on the world?

_____
_____
_____

18) Describe your childhood:

_____
_____
_____

19) What do you care about?

_____
_____
_____

20) What is your biggest fear?

_____

_____

_____

21) Do you have any secrets?

_____

_____

_____

22) How would you define yourself?

_____

_____

_____

23) What is the best thing that has ever happened to you?

_____

_____

_____

24) What is the worst thing that has ever happened to you?

_____

_____

_____

25) What would you like to accomplish in life?

_____

_____

_____

26) What do you dream about?

_____

_____

_____

27) Are you a clean or messy person? Why?

_____

_____

_____

28) What makes you laugh?

_____

_____

_____

29) What shocks or offends you?

_____

_____

_____

30) Share a funny fact about yourself:

_____

_____

_____

31) Share a deep fact about yourself:

_____

_____

_____

Author Notes on this Character

Pretend you are alone with this character. Describe them here:

_____
_____
_____
_____
_____

Write 10 words about this character as if you have known them their whole life:

_____
_____
_____
_____
_____

Now, step into this characters shoes. What do they want to accomplish in your story?

_____
_____
_____
_____
_____

Character Nine

1) What is your full name?

_____

2) How old are you and what is your gender?

_____

3) What colour is your hair; your eyes; your skin?

_____

4) Describe your physical appearance in further detail:

_____

_____

_____

5) Describe your personality:

_____

_____

_____

6) Where are you from; where did you grow up?

_____

_____

_____

7) Where do you live now?

_____

_____

_____

8) Who are your parents?

_____
_____

9) Who are your grandparents and what is their ancestral background?

_____
_____

10) Who are your friends and what do you do together?

_____
_____

11) If you are an adult, where do you work?

_____
_____

12) If you are a child, where do you go to school?

_____
_____

13) What are your likes/hobbies?

_____
_____

14) What are your dislikes?

_____
_____
_____

15) Do you have a love interest?

_____
_____
_____

16) What makes that person special to you?

_____
_____
_____

17) What is your view on the world?

_____
_____
_____

18) Describe your childhood:

_____
_____
_____

19) What do you care about?

_____
_____
_____

20) What is your biggest fear?

21) Do you have any secrets?

22) How would you define yourself?

23) What is the best thing that has ever happened to you?

24) What is the worst thing that has ever happened to you?

25) What would you like to accomplish in life?

26) What do you dream about?

_____
_____
_____

27) Are you a clean or messy person? Why?

_____
_____
_____

28) What makes you laugh?

_____
_____
_____

29) What shocks or offends you?

_____
_____
_____

30) Share a funny fact about yourself:

_____
_____
_____

31) Share a deep fact about yourself:

_____
_____
_____

AUTHOR NOTES ON THIS CHARACTER

Pretend you are alone with this character. Describe them here:

_____
_____
_____
_____
_____

Write 10 words about this character as if you have known them their whole life:

_____
_____
_____
_____
_____

Now, step into this characters shoes. What do they want to accomplish in your story?

_____
_____
_____
_____
_____

Character Ten

1) What is your full name?

_____

2) How old are you and what is your gender?

_____

3) What colour is your hair; your eyes; your skin?

_____

4) Describe your physical appearance in further detail:

_____

_____

_____

5) Describe your personality:

_____

_____

_____

6) Where are you from; where did you grow up?

_____

_____

_____

7) Where do you live now?

_____

_____

_____

8) Who are your parents?

_____

_____

_____

9) Who are your grandparents and what is their ancestral background?

_____

_____

_____

10) Who are your friends and what do you do together?

_____

_____

_____

11) If you are an adult, where do you work?

_____

_____

_____

12) If you are a child, where do you go to school?

_____

_____

_____

13) What are your likes/hobbies?

_____

_____

_____

14) What are your dislikes?

_____
_____
_____

15) Do you have a love interest?

_____
_____
_____

16) What makes that person special to you?

_____
_____
_____

17) What is your view on the world?

_____
_____
_____

18) Describe your childhood:

_____
_____
_____

19) What do you care about?

_____
_____
_____

20) What is your biggest fear?

_____
_____
_____

21) Do you have any secrets?

_____
_____
_____

22) How would you define yourself?

_____
_____
_____

23) What is the best thing that has ever happened to you?

_____
_____
_____

24) What is the worst thing that has ever happened to you?

_____
_____
_____

25) What would you like to accomplish in life?

_____
_____
_____

26) What do you dream about?

27) Are you a clean or messy person? Why?

28) What makes you laugh?

29) What shocks or offends you?

30) Share a funny fact about yourself:

31) Share a deep fact about yourself:

Author Notes on this Character

Pretend you are alone with this character. Describe them here:

_____
_____
_____
_____
_____

Write 10 words about this character as if you have known them their whole life:

_____
_____
_____
_____
_____

Now, step into this characters shoes. What do they want to accomplish in your story?

_____
_____
_____
_____
_____

Character Eleven

1) What is your full name?

2) How old are you and what is your gender?

3) What colour is your hair; your eyes; your skin?

4) Describe your physical appearance in further detail:

5) Describe your personality:

6) Where are you from; where did you grow up?

7) Where do you live now?

8) Who are your parents?

_____

_____

_____

9) Who are your grandparents and what is their ancestral background?

_____

_____

_____

10) Who are your friends and what do you do together?

_____

_____

_____

11) If you are an adult, where do you work?

_____

_____

_____

12) If you are a child, where do you go to school?

_____

_____

_____

13) What are your likes/hobbies?

_____

_____

_____

14) What are your dislikes?

_____
_____
_____

15) Do you have a love interest?

_____
_____
_____

16) What makes that person special to you?

_____
_____
_____

17) What is your view on the world?

_____
_____
_____

18) Describe your childhood:

_____
_____
_____

19) What do you care about?

_____
_____
_____

20) What is your biggest fear?

_____

_____

21) Do you have any secrets?

_____

_____

22) How would you define yourself?

_____

_____

23) What is the best thing that has ever happened to you?

_____

_____

24) What is the worst thing that has ever happened to you?

_____

_____

25) What would you like to accomplish in life?

_____

_____

_____

26) What do you dream about?

_____
_____
_____

27) Are you a clean or messy person? Why?

_____
_____
_____

28) What makes you laugh?

_____
_____
_____

29) What shocks or offends you?

_____
_____
_____

30) Share a funny fact about yourself:

_____
_____
_____

31) Share a deep fact about yourself:

_____
_____
_____

Author Notes on this Character

Pretend you are alone with this character. Describe them here:

_____
_____
_____
_____
_____
_____

Write 10 words about this character as if you have known them their whole life:

_____
_____
_____
_____
_____
_____

Now, step into this characters shoes. What do they want to accomplish in your story?

_____
_____
_____
_____
_____
_____

Character Twelve

1) What is your full name?

___

2) How old are you and what is your gender?

___

3) What colour is your hair; your eyes; your skin?

___

4) Describe your physical appearance in further detail:

___

___

___

5) Describe your personality:

___

___

___

6) Where are you from; where did you grow up?

___

___

___

7) Where do you live now?

___

___

___

8) Who are your parents?

_____
_____
_____

9) Who are your grandparents and what is their ancestral background?

_____
_____
_____

10) Who are your friends and what do you do together?

_____
_____
_____

11) If you are an adult, where do you work?

_____
_____
_____

12) If you are a child, where do you go to school?

_____
_____
_____

13) What are your likes/hobbies?

_____
_____
_____

14) What are your dislikes?

_____
_____
_____

15) Do you have a love interest?

_____
_____
_____

16) What makes that person special to you?

_____
_____
_____

17) What is your view on the world?

_____
_____
_____

18) Describe your childhood:

_____
_____
_____

19) What do you care about?

_____
_____
_____

20) What is your biggest fear?

_____
_____
_____

21) Do you have any secrets?

_____
_____
_____

22) How would you define yourself?

_____
_____
_____

23) What is the best thing that has ever happened to you?

_____
_____
_____

24) What is the worst thing that has ever happened to you?

_____
_____
_____

25) What would you like to accomplish in life?

_____
_____
_____

26) What do you dream about?

_____
_____
_____

27) Are you a clean or messy person? Why?

_____
_____
_____

28) What makes you laugh?

_____
_____
_____

29) What shocks or offends you?

_____
_____
_____

30) Share a funny fact about yourself:

_____
_____
_____

31) Share a deep fact about yourself:

_____
_____
_____

Author Notes on this Character

Pretend you are alone with this character. Describe them here:

_____

_____

_____

_____

_____

Write 10 words about this character as if you have known them their whole life:

_____

_____

_____

_____

_____

Now, step into this characters shoes. What do they want to accomplish in your story?

_____

_____

_____

_____

_____

_____

Character Thirteen

1) What is your full name?

_____

2) How old are you and what is your gender?

_____

3) What colour is your hair; your eyes; your skin?

_____

4) Describe your physical appearance in further detail:

_____

_____

_____

5) Describe your personality:

_____

_____

_____

6) Where are you from; where did you grow up?

_____

_____

_____

7) Where do you live now?

_____

_____

_____

8) Who are your parents?

_____

_____

_____

9) Who are your grandparents and what is their ancestral background?

_____

_____

_____

10) Who are your friends and what do you do together?

_____

_____

_____

11) If you are an adult, where do you work?

_____

_____

_____

12) If you are a child, where do you go to school?

_____

_____

_____

13) What are your likes/hobbies?

_____

_____

_____

14) What are your dislikes?

15) Do you have a love interest?

16) What makes that person special to you?

17) What is your view on the world?

18) Describe your childhood:

19) What do you care about?

20) What is your biggest fear?

_____
_____
_____

21) Do you have any secrets?

_____
_____
_____

22) How would you define yourself?

_____
_____
_____

23) What is the best thing that has ever happened to you?

_____
_____
_____

24) What is the worst thing that has ever happened to you?

_____
_____
_____

25) What would you like to accomplish in life?

_____
_____
_____

26) What do you dream about?

27) Are you a clean or messy person? Why?

28) What makes you laugh?

29) What shocks or offends you?

30) Share a funny fact about yourself:

31) Share a deep fact about yourself:

AUTHOR NOTES ON THIS CHARACTER

Pretend you are alone with this character. Describe them here:

_____
_____
_____
_____
_____

Write 10 words about this character as if you have known them their whole life:

_____
_____
_____
_____
_____

Now, step into this characters shoes. What do they want to accomplish in your story?

_____
_____
_____
_____
_____

Character Fourteen

1) What is your full name?

___

2) How old are you and what is your gender?

___

3) What colour is your hair; your eyes; your skin?

___

4) Describe your physical appearance in further detail:

___

___

___

5) Describe your personality:

___

___

___

6) Where are you from; where did you grow up?

___

___

___

7) Where do you live now?

___

___

___

8) Who are your parents?

_____
_____
_____

9) Who are your grandparents and what is their ancestral background?

_____
_____
_____

10) Who are your friends and what do you do together?

_____
_____
_____

11) If you are an adult, where do you work?

_____
_____
_____

12) If you are a child, where do you go to school?

_____
_____
_____

13) What are your likes/hobbies?

_____
_____
_____

14) What are your dislikes?

_____
_____
_____

15) Do you have a love interest?

_____
_____
_____

16) What makes that person special to you?

_____
_____
_____

17) What is your view on the world?

_____
_____
_____

18) Describe your childhood:

_____
_____
_____

19) What do you care about?

_____
_____
_____

20) What is your biggest fear?

_____

_____

21) Do you have any secrets?

_____

_____

22) How would you define yourself?

_____

_____

23) What is the best thing that has ever happened to you?

_____

_____

24) What is the worst thing that has ever happened to you?

_____

_____

25) What would you like to accomplish in life?

_____

_____

26) What do you dream about?

_____
_____
_____

27) Are you a clean or messy person? Why?

_____
_____
_____

28) What makes you laugh?

_____
_____
_____

29) What shocks or offends you?

_____
_____
_____

30) Share a funny fact about yourself:

_____
_____
_____

31) Share a deep fact about yourself:

_____
_____
_____

AUTHOR NOTES ON THIS CHARACTER

Pretend you are alone with this character. Describe them here:

_____
_____
_____
_____
_____
_____

Write 10 words about this character as if you have known them their whole life:

_____
_____
_____
_____
_____
_____

Now, step into this characters shoes. What do they want to accomplish in your story?

_____
_____
_____
_____
_____
_____

Character Fifteen

1) What is your full name?

_____

2) How old are you and what is your gender?

_____

3) What colour is your hair; your eyes; your skin?

_____

4) Describe your physical appearance in further detail:

_____

_____

_____

5) Describe your personality:

_____

_____

_____

6) Where are you from; where did you grow up?

_____

_____

_____

7) Where do you live now?

_____

_____

_____

8) Who are your parents?

_____

_____

_____

9) Who are your grandparents and what is their ancestral background?

_____

_____

_____

10) Who are your friends and what do you do together?

_____

_____

_____

11) If you are an adult, where do you work?

_____

_____

_____

12) If you are a child, where do you go to school?

_____

_____

_____

13) What are your likes/hobbies?

_____

_____

_____

14) What are your dislikes?

_____
_____
_____

15) Do you have a love interest?

_____
_____
_____

16) What makes that person special to you?

_____
_____
_____

17) What is your view on the world?

_____
_____
_____

18) Describe your childhood:

_____
_____
_____

19) What do you care about?

_____
_____
_____

20) What is your biggest fear?

___

21) Do you have any secrets?

___

22) How would you define yourself?

___

23) What is the best thing that has ever happened to you?

___

24) What is the worst thing that has ever happened to you?

___

25) What would you like to accomplish in life?

___

26) What do you dream about?

_____

_____

_____

27) Are you a clean or messy person? Why?

_____

_____

_____

28) What makes you laugh?

_____

_____

_____

29) What shocks or offends you?

_____

_____

_____

30) Share a funny fact about yourself:

_____

_____

_____

31) Share a deep fact about yourself:

_____

_____

_____

Author Notes on this Character

Pretend you are alone with this character. Describe them here:

Write 10 words about this character as if you have known them their whole life:

Now, step into this characters shoes. What do they want to accomplish in your story?

Character Sixteen

1) What is your full name?

2) How old are you and what is your gender?

3) What colour is your hair; your eyes; your skin?

4) Describe your physical appearance in further detail:

5) Describe your personality:

6) Where are you from; where did you grow up?

7) Where do you live now?

8) Who are your parents?

_____

_____

_____

9) Who are your grandparents and what is their ancestral background?

_____

_____

_____

10) Who are your friends and what do you do together?

_____

_____

_____

11) If you are an adult, where do you work?

_____

_____

_____

12) If you are a child, where do you go to school?

_____

_____

_____

13) What are your likes/hobbies?

_____

_____

_____

14) What are your dislikes?

15) Do you have a love interest?

16) What makes that person special to you?

17) What is your view on the world?

18) Describe your childhood:

19) What do you care about?

20) What is your biggest fear?

_____

_____

21) Do you have any secrets?

_____

_____

22) How would you define yourself?

_____

_____

23) What is the best thing that has ever happened to you?

_____

_____

24) What is the worst thing that has ever happened to you?

_____

_____

25) What would you like to accomplish in life?

_____

_____

_____

26) What do you dream about?

_____

_____

_____

27) Are you a clean or messy person? Why?

_____

_____

_____

28) What makes you laugh?

_____

_____

_____

29) What shocks or offends you?

_____

_____

_____

30) Share a funny fact about yourself:

_____

_____

_____

31) Share a deep fact about yourself:

_____

_____

_____

Author Notes on This Character

Pretend you are alone with this character. Describe them here:

_____
_____
_____
_____
_____

Write 10 words about this character as if you have known them their whole life:

_____
_____
_____
_____
_____

Now, step into this characters shoes. What do they want to accomplish in your story?

_____
_____
_____
_____
_____

CHARACTER SEVENTEEN

1) What is your full name?

2) How old are you and what is your gender?

3) What colour is your hair; your eyes; your skin?

4) Describe your physical appearance in further detail:

5) Describe your personality:

6) Where are you from; where did you grow up?

7) Where do you live now?

8) Who are your parents?

_____

_____

_____

9) Who are your grandparents and what is their ancestral background?

_____

_____

_____

10) Who are your friends and what do you do together?

_____

_____

_____

11) If you are an adult, where do you work?

_____

_____

_____

12) If you are a child, where do you go to school?

_____

_____

13) What are your likes/hobbies?

_____

_____

_____

14) What are your dislikes?

_____
_____
_____

15) Do you have a love interest?

_____
_____
_____

16) What makes that person special to you?

_____
_____
_____

17) What is your view on the world?

_____
_____
_____

18) Describe your childhood:

_____
_____
_____

19) What do you care about?

_____
_____
_____

20) What is your biggest fear?

_____

_____

_____

21) Do you have any secrets?

_____

_____

_____

22) How would you define yourself?

_____

_____

_____

23) What is the best thing that has ever happened to you?

_____

_____

_____

24) What is the worst thing that has ever happened to you?

_____

_____

_____

25) What would you like to accomplish in life?

_____

_____

_____

26) What do you dream about?

___

27) Are you a clean or messy person? Why?

___

28) What makes you laugh?

___

29) What shocks or offends you?

___

30) Share a funny fact about yourself:

___

31) Share a deep fact about yourself:

___

AUTHOR NOTES ON THIS CHARACTER

Pretend you are alone with this character. Describe them here:

_____
_____
_____
_____
_____
_____

Write 10 words about this character as if you have known them their whole life:

_____
_____
_____
_____
_____
_____

Now, step into this characters shoes. What do they want to accomplish in your story?

_____
_____
_____
_____
_____
_____

CHARACTER EIGHTEEN

1) What is your full name?

2) How old are you and what is your gender?

3) What colour is your hair; your eyes; your skin?

4) Describe your physical appearance in further detail:

5) Describe your personality:

6) Where are you from; where did you grow up?

7) Where do you live now?

8) Who are your parents?

_____

_____

_____

9) Who are your grandparents and what is their ancestral background?

_____

_____

_____

10) Who are your friends and what do you do together?

_____

_____

_____

11) If you are an adult, where do you work?

_____

_____

_____

12) If you are a child, where do you go to school?

_____

_____

_____

13) What are your likes/hobbies?

_____

_____

_____

14) What are your dislikes?

_____
_____
_____

15) Do you have a love interest?

_____
_____
_____

16) What makes that person special to you?

_____
_____
_____

17) What is your view on the world?

_____
_____
_____

18) Describe your childhood:

_____
_____
_____

19) What do you care about?

_____
_____
_____

20) What is your biggest fear?

21) Do you have any secrets?

22) How would you define yourself?

23) What is the best thing that has ever happened to you?

24) What is the worst thing that has ever happened to you?

25) What would you like to accomplish in life?

26) What do you dream about?

_____

_____

_____

27) Are you a clean or messy person? Why?

_____

_____

_____

28) What makes you laugh?

_____

_____

_____

29) What shocks or offends you?

_____

_____

_____

30) Share a funny fact about yourself:

_____

_____

_____

31) Share a deep fact about yourself:

_____

_____

_____

Author Notes on this Character

Pretend you are alone with this character. Describe them here:

_____
_____
_____
_____
_____

Write 10 words about this character as if you have known them their whole life:

_____
_____
_____
_____
_____

Now, step into this characters shoes. What do they want to accomplish in your story?

_____
_____
_____
_____
_____

Character Nineteen

1) What is your full name?

_____

2) How old are you and what is your gender?

_____

3) What colour is your hair; your eyes; your skin?

_____

4) Describe your physical appearance in further detail:

_____

_____

_____

5) Describe your personality:

_____

_____

_____

6) Where are you from; where did you grow up?

_____

_____

_____

7) Where do you live now?

_____

_____

_____

8) Who are your parents?

_____

_____

_____

9) Who are your grandparents and what is their ancestral background?

_____

_____

_____

10) Who are your friends and what do you do together?

_____

_____

_____

11) If you are an adult, where do you work?

_____

_____

_____

12) If you are a child, where do you go to school?

_____

_____

_____

13) What are your likes/hobbies?

_____

_____

_____

14) What are your dislikes?

_____
_____
_____

15) Do you have a love interest?

_____
_____
_____

16) What makes that person special to you?

_____
_____
_____

17) What is your view on the world?

_____
_____
_____

18) Describe your childhood:

_____
_____
_____

19) What do you care about?

_____
_____
_____

20) What is your biggest fear?

_____
_____
_____

21) Do you have any secrets?

_____
_____
_____

22) How would you define yourself?

_____
_____
_____

23) What is the best thing that has ever happened to you?

_____
_____
_____

24) What is the worst thing that has ever happened to you?

_____
_____
_____

25) What would you like to accomplish in life?

_____
_____
_____

26) What do you dream about?

___

27) Are you a clean or messy person? Why?

___

28) What makes you laugh?

___

29) What shocks or offends you?

___

30) Share a funny fact about yourself:

___

31) Share a deep fact about yourself:

___

AUTHOR NOTES ON THIS CHARACTER

Pretend you are alone with this character. Describe them here:

_____
_____
_____
_____
_____
_____

Write 10 words about this character as if you have known them their whole life:

_____
_____
_____
_____
_____
_____
_____

Now, step into this characters shoes. What do they want to accomplish in your story?

_____
_____
_____
_____
_____
_____

Character Twenty

1) What is your full name?

_____

2) How old are you and what is your gender?

_____

3) What colour is your hair; your eyes; your skin?

_____

4) Describe your physical appearance in further detail:

_____

_____

_____

5) Describe your personality:

_____

_____

_____

6) Where are you from; where did you grow up?

_____

_____

_____

7) Where do you live now?

_____

_____

_____

8) Who are your parents?

_____
_____
_____

9) Who are your grandparents and what is their ancestral background?

_____
_____
_____

10) Who are your friends and what do you do together?

_____
_____
_____

11) If you are an adult, where do you work?

_____
_____
_____

12) If you are a child, where do you go to school?

_____
_____
_____

13) What are your likes/hobbies?

_____
_____
_____

14) What are your dislikes?

_____

_____

_____

15) Do you have a love interest?

_____

_____

_____

16) What makes that person special to you?

_____

_____

_____

17) What is your view on the world?

_____

_____

_____

18) Describe your childhood:

_____

_____

_____

19) What do you care about?

_____

_____

_____

20) What is your biggest fear?

_____

_____

_____

21) Do you have any secrets?

_____

_____

_____

22) How would you define yourself?

_____

_____

_____

23) What is the best thing that has ever happened to you?

_____

_____

_____

24) What is the worst thing that has ever happened to you?

_____

_____

_____

25) What would you like to accomplish in life?

_____

_____

_____

26) What do you dream about?

_____
_____
_____

27) Are you a clean or messy person? Why?

_____
_____
_____

28) What makes you laugh?

_____
_____
_____

29) What shocks or offends you?

_____
_____
_____

30) Share a funny fact about yourself:

_____
_____
_____

31) Share a deep fact about yourself:

_____
_____
_____

Author Notes on this Character

Pretend you are alone with this character. Describe them here:

_____
_____
_____
_____
_____

Write 10 words about this character as if you have known them their whole life:

_____
_____
_____
_____
_____

Now, step into this characters shoes. What do they want to accomplish in your story?

_____
_____
_____
_____
_____

CHAPTER PLOTTING

Timeline

Timeline

Chapter One

_____

Chapter Title

Date/Time:

_____

_____

Setting:

_____

_____

_____

_____

_____

_____

Characters:

_____

_____

_____

_____

Voice/Point of View:

_____

_____

Chapter Summary

Expected Word Count: _____

Expected Page Count: _____

Chapter Two

Chapter Title

Date/Time:

Setting:

Characters:

Voice/Point of View:

Chapter Summary

Expected Word Count: _____

Expected Page Count: _____

Chapter Three

Chapter Title

Date/Time:

Setting:

Characters:

Voice/Point of View:

Chapter Summary

Expected Word Count: _____

Expected Page Count: _____

Chapter Four

_____

Chapter Title

Date/Time:

_____

_____

Setting:

_____

_____

_____

_____

_____

Characters:

_____

_____

_____

_____

Voice/Point of View:

_____

_____

Chapter Summary

Expected Word Count: _____

Expected Page Count: _____

CHAPTER FIVE

_____

Chapter Title

Date/Time:
_____
_____

Setting:
_____
_____
_____
_____
_____

Characters:
_____
_____
_____
_____

Voice/Point of View:
_____
_____

Chapter Summary

Expected Word Count: _____

Expected Page Count: _____

CHAPTER SIX

Chapter Title

Date/Time:
_____
_____

Setting:
_____
_____
_____
_____
_____

Characters:
_____
_____
_____
_____

Voice/Point of View:
_____
_____

Chapter Summary

Expected Word Count: _____

Expected Page Count: _____

CHAPTER SEVEN

_____

Chapter Title

Date/Time:

_____
_____

Setting:

_____
_____
_____
_____
_____

Characters:

_____
_____
_____

Voice/Point of View:

_____
_____

Chapter Summary

Expected Word Count: _____

Expected Page Count: _____

Chapter Eight

―――――――――――――
Chapter Title

Date/Time:
―――――――――――――――――――――――――――――
―――――――――――――――――――――――――――――

Setting:
―――――――――――――――――――――――――――――
―――――――――――――――――――――――――――――
―――――――――――――――――――――――――――――
―――――――――――――――――――――――――――――
―――――――――――――――――――――――――――――

Characters:
―――――――――――――――――――――――――――――
―――――――――――――――――――――――――――――
―――――――――――――――――――――――――――――

Voice/Point of View:
―――――――――――――――――――――――――――――
―――――――――――――――――――――――――――――

Chapter Summary

Expected Word Count: _____

Expected Page Count: _____

Chapter Nine

_____

Chapter Title

Date/Time:

_____
_____

Setting:

_____
_____
_____
_____
_____
_____

Characters:

_____
_____
_____
_____

Voice/Point of View:

_____
_____

Chapter Summary

Expected Word Count: _____

Expected Page Count: _____

Chapter Ten

_____

Chapter Title

Date/Time:

_____
_____

Setting:

_____
_____
_____
_____
_____

Characters:

_____
_____
_____
_____

Voice/Point of View:

_____
_____

Chapter Summary

Expected Word Count: _____

Expected Page Count: _____

Chapter Eleven

_____

Chapter Title

Date/Time:

_____
_____

Setting:

_____
_____
_____
_____

Characters:

_____
_____
_____

Voice/Point of View:

_____
_____

Chapter Summary

Expected Word Count: _____

Expected Page Count: _____

Chapter Twelve

_____

Chapter Title

Date/Time:

_____

_____

Setting:

_____

_____

_____

_____

_____

Characters:

_____

_____

_____

_____

Voice/Point of View:

_____

_____

Chapter Summary

Expected Word Count: _____

Expected Page Count: _____

Chapter Thirteen

Chapter Title

Date/Time:

Setting:

Characters:

Voice/Point of View:

Chapter Summary

Expected Word Count: _____

Expected Page Count: _____

Chapter Fourteen

Chapter Title

Date/Time:

Setting:

Characters:

Voice/Point of View:

Chapter Summary

Expected Word Count: _____

Expected Page Count: _____

Chapter Fifteen

_____

Chapter Title

Date/Time:

_____
_____

Setting:

_____
_____
_____
_____
_____

Characters:

_____
_____
_____
_____

Voice/Point of View:

_____
_____

Chapter Summary

Expected Word Count: _____

Expected Page Count: _____

Chapter Sixteen

Chapter Title

Date/Time:

_____

_____

Setting:

_____

_____

_____

_____

_____

Characters:

_____

_____

_____

_____

Voice/Point of View:

_____

_____

Chapter Summary

Expected Word Count: _____

Expected Page Count: _____

Chapter Seventeen

_____

Chapter Title

Date/Time:

_____
_____

Setting:

_____
_____
_____
_____
_____

Characters:

_____
_____
_____

Voice/Point of View:

_____
_____

Chapter Summary

Expected Word Count: _____

Expected Page Count: _____

Chapter Eighteen

_____

Chapter Title

Date/Time:

_____
_____

Setting:

_____
_____
_____
_____
_____

Characters:

_____
_____
_____

Voice/Point of View:

_____
_____

Chapter Summary

Expected Word Count: _____

Expected Page Count: _____

Chapter Nineteen

_____

Chapter Title

Date/Time:

_____

_____

Setting:

_____

_____

_____

_____

_____

Characters:

_____

_____

_____

_____

Voice/Point of View:

_____

_____

Chapter Summary

Expected Word Count: _____

Expected Page Count: _____

Chapter Twenty

Chapter Title

Date/Time:

_____
_____

Setting:

_____
_____
_____
_____
_____

Characters:

_____
_____
_____

Voice/Point of View:

_____
_____

Chapter Summary

Expected Word Count: _____

Expected Page Count: _____

Chapter Twenty-One

_____

Chapter Title

Date/Time:
_____
_____

Setting:
_____
_____
_____
_____
_____

Characters:
_____
_____
_____
_____

Voice/Point of View:
_____
_____

Chapter Summary

Expected Word Count: _____

Expected Page Count: _____

Chapter Twenty-Two

_____

Chapter Title

Date/Time:

_____
_____

Setting:

_____
_____
_____
_____
_____

Characters:

_____
_____
_____
_____

Voice/Point of View:

_____
_____

Chapter Summary

Expected Word Count: _____

Expected Page Count: _____

Chapter Twenty-Three

_____

Chapter Title

Date/Time:

_____
_____

Setting:

_____
_____
_____
_____
_____

Characters:

_____
_____
_____

Voice/Point of View:

_____
_____

Chapter Summary

Expected Word Count: _____

Expected Page Count: _____

Chapter Twenty-Four

_____
Chapter Title

Date/Time:
_____
_____

Setting:
_____
_____
_____
_____
_____

Characters:
_____
_____
_____
_____

Voice/Point of View:
_____
_____

Chapter Summary

Expected Word Count: _____

Expected Page Count: _____

Chapter Twenty-Five

_____

Chapter Title

Date/Time:

_____
_____

Setting:

_____
_____
_____
_____
_____

Characters:

_____
_____
_____
_____

Voice/Point of View:

_____
_____

Chapter Summary

Expected Word Count: _____

Expected Page Count: _____

Chapter Twenty-Six

_____

Chapter Title

Date/Time:

_____

_____

Setting:

_____

_____

_____

_____

_____

Characters:

_____

_____

_____

Voice/Point of View:

_____

_____

Chapter Summary

Expected Word Count: _____

Expected Page Count: _____

Chapter Twenty-Seven

_____

Chapter Title

Date/Time:
_____
_____

Setting:
_____
_____
_____
_____
_____

Characters:
_____
_____
_____
_____

Voice/Point of View:
_____
_____

Chapter Summary

Expected Word Count: _____

Expected Page Count: _____

Chapter Twenty-Eight

_____

Chapter Title

Date/Time:

_____
_____

Setting:

_____
_____
_____
_____
_____

Characters:

_____
_____
_____
_____

Voice/Point of View:

_____
_____

Chapter Summary

Expected Word Count: _____

Expected Page Count: _____

Chapter Twenty-Nine

_____

Chapter Title

Date/Time:
_____
_____

Setting:
_____
_____
_____
_____
_____

Characters:
_____
_____
_____

Voice/Point of View:
_____
_____

Chapter Summary

Expected Word Count: _____

Expected Page Count: _____

Chapter Thirty

_____
Chapter Title

Date/Time:
_____
_____

Setting:
_____
_____
_____
_____
_____
_____

Characters:
_____
_____
_____
_____

Voice/Point of View:
_____
_____

Chapter Summary

Expected Word Count: _____

Expected Page Count: _____

Chapter Thirty-One

Chapter Title

Date/Time:
_____
_____

Setting:
_____
_____
_____
_____
_____

Characters:
_____
_____
_____
_____

Voice/Point of View:
_____
_____

Chapter Summary

Expected Word Count: _____

Expected Page Count: _____

Chapter Thirty-Two

Chapter Title

Date/Time:

Setting:

Characters:

Voice/Point of View:

Chapter Summary

Expected Word Count: _____

Expected Page Count: _____

Yearly Writing Calendar

MONTH ONE: _____

DAY	CHAPTER	ESTIMATED	ACTUAL
1			
2			
3			
4			
5			
6			
7			
8			
9			
10			
11			
12			
13			
14			
15			
16			
17			
18			
19			
20			
21			
22			
23			
24			
25			
26			
27			
28			
29			
30			
31			

MONTH TWO: _____

DAY	CHAPTER	ESTIMATED	ACTUAL
1			
2			
3			
4			
5			
6			
7			
8			
9			
10			
11			
12			
13			
14			
15			
16			
17			
18			
19			
20			
21			
22			
23			
24			
25			
26			
27			
28			
29			
30			
31			

MONTH THREE: _____

DAY	CHAPTER	ESTIMATED	ACTUAL
1			
2			
3			
4			
5			
6			
7			
8			
9			
10			
11			
12			
13			
14			
15			
16			
17			
18			
19			
20			
21			
22			
23			
24			
25			
26			
27			
28			
29			
30			
31			

MONTH FOUR: _____

DAY	CHAPTER	ESTIMATED	ACTUAL
1			
2			
3			
4			
5			
6			
7			
8			
9			
10			
11			
12			
13			
14			
15			
16			
17			
18			
19			
20			
21			
22			
23			
24			
25			
26			
27			
28			
29			
30			
31			

MONTH FIVE: _____

DAY	CHAPTER	ESTIMATED	ACTUAL
1			
2			
3			
4			
5			
6			
7			
8			
9			
10			
11			
12			
13			
14			
15			
16			
17			
18			
19			
20			
21			
22			
23			
24			
25			
26			
27			
28			
29			
30			
31			

MONTH SIX: _____

DAY	CHAPTER	ESTIMATED	ACTUAL
1			
2			
3			
4			
5			
6			
7			
8			
9			
10			
11			
12			
13			
14			
15			
16			
17			
18			
19			
20			
21			
22			
23			
24			
25			
26			
27			
28			
29			
30			
31			

MONTH SEVEN: _____

DAY	CHAPTER	ESTIMATED	ACTUAL
1			
2			
3			
4			
5			
6			
7			
8			
9			
10			
11			
12			
13			
14			
15			
16			
17			
18			
19			
20			
21			
22			
23			
24			
25			
26			
27			
28			
29			
30			
31			

MONTH EIGHT: _____

DAY	CHAPTER	ESTIMATED	ACTUAL
1			
2			
3			
4			
5			
6			
7			
8			
9			
10			
11			
12			
13			
14			
15			
16			
17			
18			
19			
20			
21			
22			
23			
24			
25			
26			
27			
28			
29			
30			
31			

MONTH NINE: _____

DAY	CHAPTER	ESTIMATED	ACTUAL
1			
2			
3			
4			
5			
6			
7			
8			
9			
10			
11			
12			
13			
14			
15			
16			
17			
18			
19			
20			
21			
22			
23			
24			
25			
26			
27			
28			
29			
30			
31			

MONTH TEN: _____

DAY	CHAPTER	ESTIMATED	ACTUAL
1			
2			
3			
4			
5			
6			
7			
8			
9			
10			
11			
12			
13			
14			
15			
16			
17			
18			
19			
20			
21			
22			
23			
24			
25			
26			
27			
28			
29			
30			
31			

MONTH ELEVEN: _____

DAY	CHAPTER	ESTIMATED	ACTUAL
1			
2			
3			
4			
5			
6			
7			
8			
9			
10			
11			
12			
13			
14			
15			
16			
17			
18			
19			
20			
21			
22			
23			
24			
25			
26			
27			
28			
29			
30			
31			

MONTH TWELVE: _____

DAY	CHAPTER	ESTIMATED	ACTUAL
1			
2			
3			
4			
5			
6			
7			
8			
9			
10			
11			
12			
13			
14			
15			
16			
17			
18			
19			
20			
21			
22			
23			
24			
25			
26			
27			
28			
29			
30			
31			

Notes

Notes

Notes

Notes

Notes

Notes

Notes

Notes

Notes

Notes

Want more tips and inspiration...
visit us at www.novelassistantpublishing.com
and on Facebook and Twitter

www.ingramcontent.com/pod-product-compliance
Lightning Source LLC
Chambersburg PA
CBHW070130080526
44586CB00015B/1627